THE
GREATEST
DESIRE

THE GREATEST DESIRE

Daily Readings with Walter Hilton

KEVIN GOODRICH OP

DARTON · LONGMAN + TODD

First published in 2023 by
Darton, Longman and Todd Ltd
1 Spencer Court
140 – 142 Wandsworth High Street
London SW18 4JJ

The readings of Walter Hilton in this volume are excerpted
from *Walter Hilton: The Scale of Perfection*, translated and
introduced by John P. H. Clark and Rosemary Dorward.
This limited edition licensed by special permission of
Paulist Press Inc. www.paulistpress.com.

ISBN: 978-1-913657-96-3

A catalogue record for this book is available from the
British Library.

Designed and produced by Judy Linard

Printed and bound in Great Britain by
Bell & Bain, Glasgow

Contents

Introduction

This book is offered primarily for those desiring to deepen their practice of prayer, kindling a warmer and nearer relationship with God. Secondarily, it is a brief introduction to the fourteenth-century English mystic, Walter Hilton, and his most well-known work, *The Scale of Perfection* (sometimes alternatively titled, *The Ladder of Perfection*). No previous experience with Hilton or any of the fourteenth-century English mystics, such as Julian of Norwich, is necessary for a reader to benefit from this collection. In the fourteenth and fifteenth centuries Hilton was widely read. Women and men, inside and outside of monasteries, found him a helpful guide. So have many others in the over 600 years since his death in the small village of Thurgarton, England.

The selected passages can be used by readers in a variety of ways. They are designed to be read slowly, prayerfully, on a daily basis over one or two months. They could also be used as daily meditations during Lent or Advent. Regardless, a first-time reader may find it helpful to read the book through in a sitting or two before choosing to read it more slowly over time. The passages might also prove useful as short devotionals or meditations before small group sessions of prayer or study. Spiritual directors and directees may also find the excerpts useful for their work, privately, together or in group direction. Students and teachers in theology and spirituality might utilize these readings as points of departure for class discussion. I have also included suggested liturgical materials for use on Walter Hilton's Feast Day, which in the Church of England is 24 March. Lastly, I include some brief notes on Southwell and Thurgarton.

Walter Hilton was part of a movement in the fourteenth century that wrote in English as well as in Latin. Hilton wrote *The Scale* in Middle English and it is only accessible to most readers through a translation into modern English. Even in translation, Hilton's way of writing will sometimes come across to readers as archaic. As Father Robert Llewelyn wrote, 'The language of spirituality changes from one generation to another while the underlying experience remains the same.' We return to mystics like Hilton because they are witnesses to God and the human experience. We also return to them because they have preserved wisdom for us. Wisdom about life in the spirit we have forgotten.

Hilton was a near contemporary to most of the major figures associated with fourteenth-century English mysticism: Richard Rolle, Julian of Norwich, and the anonymous author of *The Cloud of Unknowing*. Like many medieval figures, we are uncertain as to the exact details of Hilton's early life. He was born around 1340. We do not have a record of his birthplace, though many scholars have suggested he was born somewhere in the East Midlands. No record of his family or early life has survived. However, he must have grown up in the shadow of the Black Death, the plague responsible for killing upwards of half the population in some areas of England. He also received an early education which prepared him to enter Cambridge, where he studied canon law.

At some point Hilton became dissatisfied with law. He sought a life of intentional prayer, contemplation, and religious observance. He began as a hermit – a solitary – before joining the community of Augustinian canons in the village of Thurgarton. Thurgarton is about an hour's walk from the Minster Church in the town of Southwell, in present day Nottinghamshire. In Thurgarton, Hilton wrote most of his major works, including *The Scale of Perfection*. Medieval canons were like monks in that they lived in community, took vows, and gathered daily for prayer (e.g. Matins and Evensong). They also ministered to the needs of the surrounding community. *The Scale of Perfection* consists of two volumes, though in most editions, medieval and modern, they are almost always included together. The first volume is written to an anchoress – a solitary. The second volume may have been written to a wider contemplative audience. In both volumes, Hilton is providing spiritual direction. Direction to readers about seeking union with God.

In selecting passages for this book I have attempted to give a broad overview of Hilton's topics throughout *The Scale*. The meditative nature of shorter passages that are important to this volume make it impossible to give a full and detailed overview of *The Scale*'s contents. In order to keep passages to one page and intelligible to readers, I have taken mostly minor liberties with the translation of the text. This has sometimes required adding a brief phrase or word or omitting a phrase or section from a given chapter. The passage headers are mine, though often I have simply shorted the standard chapter titles found in *The Scale*. I have omitted the use of dots or ellipses because I believe this these would take away from the reader's experience. This meditative volume is not intended as a replacement for a complete edition of the *Scale*. There are several of these available. I recommend the John Clark and Rosemary Dorward edition from *The Classics of Western Spirituality* series by Paulist Press. Paulist Press has gracious given permission to use that edition's translation in this book.

In *The Scale*, Walter Hilton writes to an anchoress. A woman who has committed herself to a lifetime of prayer in pursuit of union with God. His wisdom and insight are applicable to those, like her, formally seeking the contemplative life within a monastery. However, his insights are also applicable to those desiring a contemplative experience in the hustle and bustle of an active life. This also includes those who aren't sure what kind of life they are seeking, but know they have a desire to experience more of God, more of their faith and more of the spiritual power of love. Hilton writes, 'For prayer is nothing but a desire of the heart rising into God.' May God grant you that desire in increasing measure so that your heart may rise ever higher into that great mystery of love.

Daily readings from
The Scale of Perfection

Turning to God

For you must know that a turning of the body to God, not followed by the heart, is only a figure and likeness of virtues, and not the reality. Therefore any man or woman is wretched who neglects all the inward keeping of the self in order to fashion only an outward form and semblance of holiness, in dress, in speech and in bodily actions; observing the deeds of others and judging their faults; considering himself to be something when he is nothing at all; and so deceiving himself.

Do not behave like that but turn your heart together with your body first of all to God, and fashion yourself within to his likeness, through humility and charity and other spiritual virtues; and then you will truly have turned to him.

Love and charity

�֍

Active life lies in love and charity shown outwardly in good bodily works, in the fulfilment of God's commandments and of the seven works of mercy – bodily and spiritual – toward one's fellow Christians. This way of life belongs to all secular people who have riches and plenty of worldly goods, and also to those with either standing, office, or charge over others and having wealth to spend, whether they are clergy or laity, temporal or spiritual.

In general, all secular people are bound to fulfil this obligation according to their power and ability, as reason and discretion require; if anyone has a great deal, do a great deal; if he has little, do little; and if he has nothing, then let him have the will to do good. These are the works of active life. And although these works are active, nevertheless they greatly help a person and dispose him in the beginning to come to the contemplative life, if they are used with discretion.

The first part of contemplation

*

The first part of contemplation lies in the knowledge of God and the things of the spirit, acquired by reason, by the teaching of man and the study of holy scripture, without the spiritual affection or inward savor felt by the special gift of the Holy Spirit. This part belongs especially to some great scholars who by long study and labor in holy scripture come to this knowledge – more, or less, according to the subtly of their natural wit and their perseverance in study, upon the basis of the general gift given by God to everyone who has the use of reason.

This knowledge is good, and it may be called a part of contemplation in as much as it is a sight of truth and a knowledge of spiritual things. Yet this kind of knowledge is common to good and bad, because it may be had without charity. Nevertheless, if those who have this knowledge keep themselves in such humility and charity as they have and flee worldly and carnal sins as they are able, it is a good way for them, strongly disposing them to true contemplation, if they desire and pray devoutly for the grace of the Holy Spirit. Knowledge by itself puffs up the heart into pride but mix it with charity and then it turns to edification.

The second part
of contemplation

The second part of contemplation lies principally in affection, without the understanding of spiritual things; this is commonly for simple and unlearned people who give themselves entirely to devotion, and it is felt in the following way. Sometimes a man or woman meditating on God feels a fervor of love and spiritual sweetness in the remembrance of Jesus' passion or he or she feels great trust in the goodness and mercy of God for the forgiveness of their sins or else in prayer they feel the thought of their hearts draw up from all earthly things, streamed together with all its powers as it rises into our Lord by fervent desire and with spiritual delight.

Nevertheless, in that time the man or woman has no open sight for the understanding of spiritual things or into the particular mysteries of holy scriptures; only it seems for the time that nothing pleases the man or woman so much as praying because of the savor, delight, and comfort they find in it. They cannot well explain what it is but feel it plainly; for from it spring many sweet tears, burning desires and mournings, which scour and cleanse the heart from all the filth of sin and make it melt into a wonderful sweetness of Jesus Christ – obedient, supple and ready to fulfil all God's will.

Active life and contemplation

✴

Those in active life may by grace have the second part of contemplation, that is affection, when they are visited by our Lord, just as strongly and as fervently as those who give themselves entirely to the contemplative life and have this gift; but it does not last so long. In the same way, this feeling in its fervor does not always come when one wishes, and it does not last very long; it comes and goes as God wills. Therefore, whoever has it should humble themselves and thank God.

Let them keep it secret except from their confessor or director and hold it as long as they can with discretion; and when it is withdrawn, let them not dread too much, but stand in faith and in meek hope, with patient waiting until it comes again. This is a little tasting of the sweetness in the love of God about which David speaks thus in the Psalter: *Taste and see the sweetness of the Lord* (Psalm 34:8).

The third part of contemplation

The third part of contemplation, which is as perfect as can be here, lies both in cognition and in affection: that is to say, in the knowing and perfect loving of God. That is when a person's soul is first cleansed from all sins and reformed to the image of Jesus by completeness of virtues, and afterward is visited and taken up from all earthly and fleshly affections, from vain thoughts and imaginations of all bodily things, and is as if forcibly ravished out of the bodily senses.

Then it is illumined by the grace of the Holy Spirit to see intellectually the Truth, which is God, and also spiritual things, with a soft, sweet burning love for him – so perfectly that by the rapture of this love the soul is for the time united and conformed to the image of the Trinity. The beginning of this contemplation may be felt in this life, but the fullness of it is kept in the bliss of heaven.

St Paul says this of such union and comforming: '*But anyone united to the Lord becomes one spirit with him*' (1 Corinthians 6:17). That is to say, if anyone is fastened to God by the rapture of love, the God and the soul are not two, but both are one – not in flesh, but one in spirit – and certainly in this union that marriage is made between God and the soul which shall never be broken.

Personal visions and revelations

By what I have said you will to some extent understand that visions or revelations of any kind of spirit, appearing in the body or in the imagination, asleep or awake, or any other feeling in the bodily senses made in spiritual fashion – either in sound by the ear, or tasting in the mouth, or smelling to the nose, or else any heat that can be felt like fire glowing and warming the breast or any other part of the body, or anything that be felt by bodily sense, however comforting and pleasing it may be – these are not truly contemplation.

They are only simple and secondary – though they are good – compared with spiritual virtues and the spiritual knowledge and loving of God. For in virtues and in the knowledge of God with love there is no deceit, but all such feelings, may be either good, the work of a good angel, or they may be deceitful: the contrivance of a wicked angel when he transfigures himself into an angel of light. Therefore they are not to be greatly desired or carelessly received, unless a soul can by the spirit of discretion know the good from the evil, and so escape beguilement. St John speaks in this way, *Do not believe every spirit, but first to try whether he is from God or not* (1 John 4:1).

Virtues begin in reason and end in love

Now I have told you a little about contemplation with the intention that you might know it and set it as a beacon before the sight of your soul, desiring all through your life to come to any part of it by the grace of our Lord Jesus Christ. This is the conforming of a soul to be like God, which may not be achieved unless it is first reformed by the fullness of virtues, turned into affection; and that is when somebody loves a virtue because it is good in itself. There is many a person that has virtues, such as lowliness, patience, charity toward their fellow Christians and so on, only in their reason and will, but without any spiritual delight or love in them.

Often such a person feels grudging, sad and bitter as they practice them, stirred only by reason and the fear of God. This person has virtues in their reason and will, but not the love of them in affection. But when by the grace of Jesus and by spiritual and bodily exercise the reason is turned into light and the will into love, then a person has virtues in affection, That is to say, the virtues which were at first hard to practice are now turned into real delight and savor, as happens when someone enjoys themselves in patience, humility, purity, sobriety and charity, as much as in any pleasures.

Who should censure people's faults and who should not

It is not your duty or that of anyone else having the state and purpose of contemplative life to leave off keeping watch on yourself and to rebuke others for their faults, except in very great need and when someone would perish without your reproof. It is for those who are active and have authority and charge over others, as have prelates, pastors and people of that kind.

They are bound by their office and by the way of charity to see, search out and pass righteous judgments on the faults of others not out of desire and delight in pursuing them but only in need, with fear of God and in his name, for the love and salvation of their souls.

Others who are active and have no charge over others are obliged by charity to rebuke people for their faults only when the sin is mortal, when it cannot well be corrected by anyone else, and when they believe the sinner would be amended by their reproof; otherwise it is better to desist. Therefore you must never judge other people or willingly conceive any evil suspicion against them.

Acquire humility

There is danger for you in deliberately exalting and lifting yourself in thought above any other person, for our Lord says, *Whoever exalts himself shall be humbled and whoever humbles himself shall be exalted* (Matthew 23:12). This part of humility you must have when you begin: by this and by grace you will come to the fullness of it and of all other virtues; for whoever has one virtue, has all. Whatever the amount of humility you have, you will have as much charity, patience and other virtues, though they may not be shown outwardly.

Take pains, then, to acquire humility and hold it, for it is the first and last of all virtues. It is the first because it is the foundation, as St Augustine says: If you think to build a tall house of virtues, first plan for yourself a deep foundation of humility. It is also the last, for it saves and keeps all virtues, as St Gregory says: He who gathers virtues without humility is like someone preparing and carrying powdered spices in the wind. However many good deeds you may do – fasting, waking, or any other good work – if you have no humility, you do nothing.

For lack of humility

✳

Hypocrites do not feel this humility either in good will or in affection, but their hearts and loins are too dry and cold – alien to the soft feeling of this virtue – and inasmuch as they suppose themselves to have it, they are further from it. They show outward humility in clothing, in holy speech and in lowly bearing and (as it seems) in many great virtues of body and spirit; but nevertheless in the will and affection of their heart, where humility should be first of all, it is only pretended, for they despise and think nothing of all others, who will not do as they do or teach. They consider them either fools through ignorance or blinded by their carnal way of life, and therefore in their own sight they lift themselves on high above all the rest.

They think that they live better than others, surpassing other people in both knowledge and in spiritual feeling. From this view within them arises a great delight in their hearts through which they honor and praise themselves as if there were nobody else. They praise and thank God with their lips, but in their hearts they steal like thieves the honor and thanksgiving from God and set it upon themselves; and so they have no humility either in will or in feeling.

What things to believe

Steadfastly believe that you are ordained by our Lord to be saved as one of his chosen, by his mercy; and do not budge from this belief whatever you hear or see, whatever temptation you are in. Although you feel that you are so great a wretch that you are worthy to sink into hell, because you do nothing good and do not serve God as you should; yet hold yourself in this faith, and in this hope, and ask mercy: and all shall be very well.

Yes – and even if all the devils of hell appeared to you, waking or sleeping, in bodily form, saying that you should not be saved, or all people living on earth, or all the angels of heaven (if that might be) told you the same thing, you should not believe them or be moved much from this faith and hope of salvation. For this reason it seems to me helpful for every creature to have trust in salvation.

A stable intention

Have from the beginning a whole and stable intention, that is to say, a whole will and desire only to please God: for that is charity, without which everything you do would be nothing. You shall fix your purpose in a continual search and labor to please God, never willingly leaving the good occupation of body or spirit. For with regard to your bodily nature, it is good to use discretion in eating, drinking and sleeping, and in every kind of bodily penance either in prolonged vocal prayer or in bodily feeling from great fervor of devotion – as in weeping or the like – and in spiritual imagining as well when one feels no grace.

In all these kind of work it is good to keep discretion, perhaps by breaking off sometimes; for moderation is best. But in the destruction of sin by guarding your heart, and in the perpetual desire for virtues and the glory of heaven and for possession of the spiritual knowledge and love of God – in these hold to no mean, for the more there is of this, the better. I do not say that this intention is necessary for salvation, but I think it profitable, and if you keep it you shall advance more in virtue in one year than you could without it in seven.

Make an offering

I have also spoken of the beginning: what you need to have, such as humility, a sure faith, and a whole intention toward God, on which ground you shall set your spiritual house by prayer and meditation and other spiritual virtues. Whether you pray or meditate, or do anything else – good by grace, or bad through your own frailty – or whatever you feel, see or hear, smell or taste, outwardly by your bodily senses or inwardly in the imagination or feeling of your reason or knowledge, bring it all within the faith and rules of holy church.

Cast it all with humility and the fear of God into the fire of desire and offer it to God. I tell you truthfully, that this offering will be very pleasing in the sight of our Lord Jesus, and the smoke of that fire will smell sweet before his face. That is to say, draw all that you feel within the faith of holy church, break yourself in humility, and offer the desire of your heart to your Lord Jesus alone, to have him and nothing else but him. St Paul taught us when he said: *Whether you eat or drink, or whatever kind of work you do, do it all in the name of our Lord Jesus Christ, forsaking yourself, and offer it up to him* (1 Corinthians 10:31).

How prayer is useful

Prayer is profitable, and a useful means of getting purity of heart through the destruction of sin and the reception of virtues. Not that you should by your prayer tell our Lord what you desire, for he knows all your needs well enough; but by your prayer make yourself able and ready like a clean vessel ready to receive the grace that our Lord will freely give you, and this cannot be felt until you are purified by the fire of desire in devout prayer. Although it is true that prayer is not the cause for which our Lord gives grace, nevertheless it is a way by which grace, freely given, comes to a soul.

But now perhaps you want to know how you should pray, and on what you should set the point of your thought in your prayer, and also what prayer would be best for you to use. I would answer the first like this. When you have woken up from your sleep and are ready to pray, you will feel yourself carnal and heavy, slipping down all the time into vain thoughts, either of dreams, or of fancies, or of irrational concerns of the world or your flesh. Then you need to quicken your heart with prayer and stir it as much as you can to some devotion.

The Church's prayer

Concerning vocal prayer it seems to me that for you who are bound by custom and rule to say Matins, Evensong, and the other hours of prayer; it is most useful to say these as devoutly as you can. For when you say your Matins you also say the Our Father, and to stir you to more devotion it was further laid down that psalms, hymns, and other similar pieces made by the Holy Spirit should be said as well (such as the Hail Mary). Therefore you shall not say them greedily or carelessly as if you resented being tied to them.

Rather, you shall collect your affection and your thoughts to say them more steadfastly and more devoutly than any other special prayer of devotion. After these, if you wish, you may use other prayers, the best being those in which you feel the most savor and spiritual comfort. A person needs a firm staff to hold them up if they cannot run easily by spiritual prayer because their feet of knowing and loving are infirm through sin. This staff is the special spoken prayer ordained by God and holy church to help people's souls. By this prayer the soul of a person who is always falling down into worldly thoughts and affections will be lifted up as by a staff.

Spoken prayer

Another kind of prayer is spoken, but without any particular set words, and this is when a man or woman feels the grace of devotion by the gift of God, and in his or her devotion speaks to God as if he were bodily present. The man or woman uses the words that best match their inward stirrings for the time and that have come to their mind following the different concerns they feel in their heart, rehearsing either their sins or the malice and tricks of the Enemy, or else the goodness and mercy of God.

And with that the man or woman cries to our Lord for succor and help, with the desire of their heart and the words of their mouth, like a man in peril among his enemies, or like someone in sickness showing her sores to God as a doctor, and saying thus: (Ah, Lord deliver me from my enemies); (Psalm 59:1) or else thus: (Ah, Lord heal my soul, for I have sinned against you); (Psalm 41: 4) or anything similar that comes to mind. And also it seems to the person praying there is so much goodness, grace and mercy in God that they are glad to praise and thank him with great affection from the heart, using such words as are fit for the glorifying and praise of God.

Silent prayer

✳

Yet another kind of prayer is only in the heart, without speaking, and with great rest of body and soul. Anyone who is to pray well in this way needs to have a pure heart, for it belongs to those men and women who by long labor of body and soul – or else by such sharp striking of love come into rest of spirit, so that their affection is turned into spiritual savor, and so that they can pray in their heart continually, glorifying and praising God, without great hindrance from temptations or vanities.

The fire of love shall always be alight in the soul of a devout man or woman, which is the altar of our Lord; and every day in the morning the priest shall lay sticks and nourish the fire. That is to say, This man or woman shall nourish the fire of love in their heart with holy psalms, pure thoughts, and fervent desires, so that it never goes out.

Distractions in prayer

When you want to have the intention of your heart held upward to God in prayer, you feel so many vain thoughts of the things you have done or will do, or of other people's actions, with many other such matters hindering and vexing you, that you can feel neither savor nor rest in your prayer nor devotion in what you are saying.

Often the more you labor to control your heart, the further it is from you, and sometimes the harder it is from beginning to end, so that you feel that everything you do is lost. When you are about to pray, make your intention and your will at the beginning as complete and as pure toward God as you can, briefly in your mind, and then begin and do as you can.

And however badly you are hindered from your first resolve, do not be too fearful, or too angry with yourself, or impatient. Instead, trust confidently in the mercy of our Lord that he will make it good and if you do so, all shall be well. For there are many souls who are unable ever to find rest of heart in prayer, but struggle with their thoughts all their lifetime, hindered and troubled by them. If they keep themselves in humility and charity in other respects, they shall have a very great reward in heaven for their great labor.

Against temptations

✴

A remedy for temptations may be as follows. First, that you steadfastly believe that all this sorrow and travail that you suffer in such temptations, which to an ignorant person seems to be desertion by God, is neither rejection by God nor desertion, but trial for your good: either to cleanse sins already committed, or to give you a great increase in your reward, or great disposition to abundant grace, if only you will endure and suffer awhile and stand fast, so that you do not willfully turn again to sin.

Another remedy is not to fear or take to heart such malicious stirrings of despair or blasphemy, or disbelief in the sacrament, or any other similar things that might be horrible to hear, for the feeling of these temptations defiles the soul no more than if one heard a dog bark or a felt a flea bite. They trouble the soul but do not harm it, if you have the will to despise them and think nothing of them.

Striving with temptations

✡

It is not good to strive with them so as to put them out by force; for the more that people struggle against such thoughts, the more they cling to them; therefore, as far as possible they should withdraw their attention from them as if they cared nothing for them and direct it to some other occupation. And if they will always hang upon them, then it is good for them not to be angry or despondent when they feel them, but with a good trust in God to bear them like a bodily pain. In addition to this, it is good for them to show their hearts to some wise person at the beginning, before these things have taken root.

They should leave their own judgment to follow this wise person's advice: but not to show them lightly to any unlearned or worldly person who has never felt such temptations. For through this person's ignorance a simple soul might easily be brought to despair. When you are brought so low by laboring in temptation that it seems there is no help or comfort for you, but as if you were a man or woman destroyed, yet pray to God, and indeed you shall suddenly spring up as the day star in gladness of heart.

Work as you can

We can always desire the best, but we cannot always perform the best, for we have not received that grace. A hound that runs after the hare only because he sees other hounds running will rest when he is tired, and turn back; but if he runs because he sees the hare, he will not flag for weariness until he has it. It is just the same spiritually. If anyone has a grace, however small, and decides to stop working with it and make himself labor at another that he does not yet have, only because he sees or hears that others are doing so, he may indeed run for a while until he is weary; and then he will turn home again.

But when anyone works with such grace as he has while humbly and persistently desiring more, and later feels his heart stirred to follow the grace which he has desired; he can safely run, provided he keeps humility. And therefore desire from God as much as you can – without moderation or discretion – of all that belongs to his love and the bliss of heaven, for whoever knows how best to desire from God shall have the most feeling of him; but work as you can, and call for mercy on what you cannot.

Know Thyself

There is one useful and deserving task on which to labor, a plain highway to contemplation, as far as can lie in human effort: and that is for a person to go into himself or herself to know their own soul and its powers, its fairness and its foulness. Through looking inward you will be able to see the honor and dignity it ought to have from the nature of the first making: and you will see too the misery into which you have fallen through sin.

From this sight there will come into your heart a great desire with great longing to recover that dignity and honor which you have lost. You will also feel a loathing and horror of yourself, with a great will to destroy and suppress yourself and everything that hinders you from that dignity and joy. This is a task for the spirit, hard and sharp in the beginning for anyone who will work vigorously in it, for it is a labor in the soul against the ground of all sins, small or great and this ground is nothing but a false disordered love of a person for themselves.

Be saved

However great a wretch you may be, and however much sin you have committed, forsake yourself and all your works, good and bad. Cry for mercy and ask only salvation by virtue of our Lord's precious passion, humbly, and with trust, and no doubt you shall have it. You shall be saved from this original sin and every other that you have done.

And not only you but all souls who put their trust in his passion and humble themselves, acknowledging their wickedness, asking for mercy and forgiveness and the fruit of this precious passion alone, and submitting themselves to the sacraments of holy church. Although they may have been encumbered with sin all their lives without ever feeling any spiritual savor or sweetness or spiritual knowledge of God, in this faith and in their goodwill, they shall be saved and come to the bliss of heaven by the power of this precious passion of our Lord Jesus Christ.

The image of the Trinity

Although we could never acquire it here in its fullness, yet we must desire while living here to recover a figure and a likeness of that dignity, so that by grace our soul might be reformed as it were in a shadow to the image of the Trinity, which we had by nature and afterward shall have fully in glory. For that is the life which is truly contemplative to begin here, in that feeling of love and spiritual knowledge of God, by opening of the spiritual eye; and it shall never be lost or taken away; but the same shall be fulfilled in another way in the bless of heaven.

I do not say that while living here you can recover such whole or perfect purity, innocence, or knowing and loving God as you had at first or as you shall have; neither can you escape all the wretchedness and pains of sin, or entirely destroy and quench the false vain love of yourself while living in mortal flesh, or avoid all venial sins. But if you cannot quench it altogether, I would wish you partly to abate it, and come as close to that purity as you can.

What you seek

✶

I shall speak one word for all that you shall seek, desire and find, for in that word is all that you have lost. This word is Jesus. I do not mean the word Jesus painted on the wall, written in letters in the book, formed by the lips with sound from the mouth, or fashioned in the heart by labor of the mind, for this is the way someone out of charity can find him; but I mean Jesus, all goodness, everlasting bliss; your God, your Lord, and your salvation.

Then by whatever kind of prayer, meditation, or occupation you can have the greatest desire for him and the most feeling of him; by that occupation you seek him best, and best find him. Although it may happen that you feel him in devotion or in knowing, or in any other gift, whatever it may be, do not rest in it as though you had fully found Jesus, but always be longing for Jesus more and more, to find him better. For whatever you feel of him, however much, you have not yet found him fully as he is.

Finding Jesus

So now see the courtesy and mercy of Jesus. You have lost him, but where? Certainly in your house, that is, in your soul. He is in you, even though he is lost from you, but you are not in him till you have found him. This, then, was his mercy; that he would allow himself to be lost only where he can be found. There is no need to run to Rome or Jerusalem to look for him there but turn your thought into your own soul where he is and look for him there.

Jesus sleeps in your heart spiritually as he once slept bodily when he was in the ship with his disciples; but they awoke him for fear of perishing, and at once he saved them from the tempest. Do the same yourself; stir him up with prayer and awaken him by crying with desire, and he will soon get up and help you.

Humility and charity

For this reason prepare yourself to put on Our Lord's likeness – that is the humility and charity which are his garments – and then he will want to know you familiarly and show you his mystery. There is no virtue you can practise – no work you can do – able to make you resemble our Lord without humility and charity, for these especially are the garments of God.

In the gospel, where our Lord speaks of humility thus: *Learn from me, for I am mild and meek in heart* (Matthew 11:29). Also, he speaks of charity: *This is my commandment, that you love one another as I have loved you* (John 13:34).

The image of sin

This image of sin is a false disordered love for yourself. Out of this love there come all kinds of sin in seven rivers, which are these: pride, envy, wrath, sloth, covetousness, gluttony and lust. Every kind of sin runs out by one of these rivers, driving out or lessening the fervor of charity. Now you can feel by groping that this image is not nothing, but full of wretchedness, for it is a great spring of love for yourself, with seven rivers of the kind I have mentioned.

A man had a stinking well in his garden with many small streams. He went and stopped the streams and left the spring whole, thinking all was safe, but the water sprang up at the bottom of the well and lay there stagnant in such quantity that it corrupted all the beauty of his garden; and yet no water was running out. It can be just the same with you. If it happens that by grace you have thoroughly stopped the rivers of the image of sin outwardly, it is good; but, unless you stop and cleanse this image inwardly as much as you can, it will corrupt all the flowers in the garden of your soul.

Different rewards

You shall understand that in the bliss of heaven there are two rewards our Lord gives to chosen souls. One is supreme and principal, as is the love and knowledge of God according to the measure of best and highest, for it is God himself, and it is common to all the souls that are to be saved, in whatever state or degree they are living in holy church: more or less, according to the quantity and greatness of their charity.

For the person that here in this life loves God most in charity shall have the most reward in the bliss of heaven, whatever degree he may be in, whether layman or priest, secular or religious, for he shall most love God and know him, and that is the supreme reward. And as for this reward, it will happen that some secular man or woman – lord or lady – knight or squire, merchant or ploughman, or whatever degree he is in, man or woman – shall have more than some priest or friar, monk or canon, or enclosed anchoress. Any why? Because that person loved God more.

Envy and wrath

The branches of wrath and envy are these: hatred, evil, suspicion, false and unfounded judgments, sullen resentment rising in your heart, contempt, backbiting, irrational blame, insult, unkindness, displeasure, bitterness and vexation against those that despise you or speak evil of you; with gladness at their distress and hardness against sinful people and others who will not behave as you feel they should; and with great desire in your heart (under the appearance of charity and righteousness) that they should be well-punished and chastised for their sins.

This stirring seems good. Nevertheless, if you look into it well you will sometimes find it more carnal against the person than spiritual against the sin. You are to love the person, however sinful they may be; and you shall hate the sin, in every person, whoever they may be. Woe to those who say that evil is good and good evil, putting light for darkness and bitter for sweet. So do all those who, thinking that they hate the sin, hate the person instead of the sin, when they should hate the sin of their fellow Christians and love the person.

It is hard to love people

There is no difficulty in waking and fasting until your head and body ache, or in going to Rome and Jerusalem on your bare feet, or in rushing about and preaching as if you wanted to convert everybody with your sermons. Neither is it hard to build churches or chapels or to feed the poor and build hospitals. But is a very difficult thing for someone to love his fellow Christians in charity, and wisely to hate their sin while loving the person.

For although it may be true that all the works I have mentioned are good in themselves, nevertheless they are common to good people and to bad, many could do them if they wanted to and had the wherewithal. Therefore, I regard it as no great feat to do what everyone can do; but to love one's fellow Christians in charity and hate their sin can be done only by good people, who have it by the gift of God and not by their own labor, as St Paul says: Love and charity is diffused in your hearts by the Holy Spirit, who is given to you, and therefore it is more precious, and the rarer to come by (Romans 5:5).

Love your enemies

The more you are stirred against the person and the greater your ill-will, the further you are from perfect charity toward your fellow Christians; the less you are stirred, the nearer you are to charity. If you are not stirred against the person – either outwardly by an angry face, or in your own heart by any secret hatred, to despise or judge them but the more shame and disgrace they cause you in word and deed, the more pity and compassion you have for them, as you would for a man or woman out of their mind; if you feel you cannot find it in your heart to hate this person but you pray for them, help them, and desire this person's amendment.

Doing this not only with your mouth as hypocrites know how to do, but with the affection of love in your heart – then you have perfect charity toward your fellow Christian. St Stephen had this charity perfectly when he prayed for those that stoned him to death, and Christ counselled it for all who wanted to be his perfect followers and when he said: *Love your enemies and do good to them that hate you; pray for those who persecute and slander you* (Matthew 5:44). Therefore if you want to follow Christ, be like him in this craft; learn to love your enemies.

How to speak with people

✳

Like every man and woman you are bound to love your fellow Christian, first of all in your heart and also in need. Therefore, if anyone wants to speak with you, whoever they are and of whatever their rank, be ready quickly with a good will to know what they want. You may be in prayer or devotion, so that you grudge breaking off because you feel you should not leave God for any person's talk. I feel it is not so, for if you are wise you shall not leave God, but you shall find and see God in your fellow Christian just as well as in your prayer.

If you knew how to love your fellow Christian, speaking to them discreetly should be no hindrance to you. Whoever comes to you, ask humbly what they want and if they come to tell of you their trouble and to be comforted by what you say, hear them gladly and let them say what they want, to ease their own heart; and when they have finished, comfort them if you know how, kindly and charitably, and soon break off. Then after that, if they fall into idle tales or vanities of the world or of other people's doings, say little in reply and do not feed this person's talk, and they will soon feel bored and soon take their leave.

Break the image of sin

This image of sin is borne by you and every person, whoever they may be, until by the grace of Jesus it is to some extent destroyed and broken down. Although in the beginning a man was made stable and steadfast in the image of God, yet because of sin, living in this world he proceeds in this image of sin, by which he is made unstable and troubled in vain. Then what are you do with this image? I answer you with a word that the crowd spoke to Pilate about Christ: 'Crucify him.' Take this body of sin and put it upon the cross. That is to say, break down this image and slay the false love of sin in yourself. Who shall help you to break down this image? Certainly, your Lord Jesus. In his strength and in his name you shall break down this idol of sin. Pray to him diligently and with desire, and he shall help you.

Bear the image of Jesus

You shall be formed again to the image of the man Jesus by humility and charity, and then you shall be fully shaped to the image of Jesus God, living here in a shadow of contemplation, and in the glory of heaven by the fullness of truth. St Paul speaks thus of this shaping to the likeness of Christ.

My dear children, whom I bear as a woman bears a child until Christ is again shaped in you (Galatians 4:19). You have conceived Christ through faith and he has life in you inasmuch as you have a good will and a desire to serve and please him, but he is not yet fully formed in you, nor you in him, by the fullness of charity. And therefore St Paul bore you and me and others in the same way with travail as a woman bears a child, until the time that Christ has his full shape in us, and we in him.

The passion of Christ

The passion of our Lord and this precious death are the ground of all the reforming of a person's soul, without which it could never have been reformed to Christ's likeness or come to the glory of heaven. Now it is true that by virtue of this precious passion the burning sword of the cherub that drove Adam out of Paradise is now put away, and the eternal gates of heaven are open to every person who wants to enter there.

For Jesus is both God and king of heaven, equal to the glory of the Father, and as a man he is porter at the gate, ready to receive every soul that wishes to be reformed to his likeness here in his life. For now every soul may be reformed to the likeness of God if they will, since the trespass is forgiven and amends made through Jesus. Nevertheless, not all souls have the profit or the fruit of this precious passion, neither are they reformed to Christ likeness.

Reforming is of two kinds

This reforming is of two kinds: one is in faith alone, and the other is in faith and in feeling. The first, which is reforming in faith alone, is sufficient for salvation; the second worthy of surpassing reward in the bliss of heaven. The first may be gained easily and in a short time; the second not so, but through length of time and great spiritual labor. The first can be had together with the feeling of the image of sin, for though a person feels nothing in themselves, but all stirrings of sinful desires, notwithstanding that feeling, they may be reformed in faith to the likeness of God.

But the second reforming drives out the enjoyment and feeling of worldly desires and allow no such spots to remain in this image. The first reforming is only for souls beginning and proficient, and for people in active life; the second is for perfect souls and contemplatives. By the first reforming the image of sin is not destroyed but it is left as if all whole in feeling; but the second reforming destroys the old feelings of this image of sin and brings into the soul new gracious feelings through the working of the Holy Spirit. The first is good; the second is better, but the third, which is the bliss of heaven, is best of all.

The confession of sin

Any Christian man or woman who has lost the likeness of God through mortal sin, breaking God's commandments; if through the touch of grace they forsakes their sin with sorrow and contrition of heart, and fully intend to amend and turn to God and to good living, and with this intention receives the sacrament of penance if they can – of if they cannot, has the will to do it – then the soul of this man or woman, deformed as it was before to the likeness of the devil through mortal sin, is now by the sacrament of penance restored and shaped again to the image of our Lord God.

This is a great courtesy of our Lord's, and an infinite mercy, who so easily forgives all kinds of sin and so promptly gives abundant grace to a sinful soul that asks him for mercy. Our Lord does not wait for great penance to be done or for painful bodily suffering before he forgives it, but he asks for a loathing of sin and a full forsaking by the will of the soul, for the love of him, and a turning to him of the heart. When God sees this, without any delay he forgives the sin and reforms the soul to his likeness. The sin is forgiven.

Mercy for troubled consciences

In this reforming that is only in faith the greater part of chosen souls lead their life, who steadfastly set their will to flee every kind of mortal sin, to hold themselves in love and charity toward their fellow Christians, and to keep the commandments of God as far as they know. When it so happens that the stirrings of wickedness and evil intentions rise in their hearts – of pride, envy, anger, lust or any other capital sin – they withstand them and strive against them with resolute displeasure, so that these wicked purposes are not followed by deeds.

Nevertheless, if they carelessly fall, as it were against their will through frailty or ignorance, at once their conscience troubles them and pains them so grievously that they can have no rest until they have confessed and can receive forgiveness. Indeed I consider that all these souls living so are reformed in faith to the image of God; and if they live in this reforming and are found in it at the hour of their death, they shall be saved and come to full reforming in the bliss of heaven, even though they could never have spiritual feeling or inward or special grace or devotion in all their lifetime.

Make no friendship with sin

Therefore a soul needs always to be striving and fighting against wicked stirrings from this image of sin, and to make no agreement or friendship with it, to be obedient to its irrational biddings, for if one does, he or she deceives themselves. But in truth if a soul strives with them there is not much fear in this consenting, for strife breaks peace and false accord. It is good for a man or woman to have peace with everything except with the devil and with this image of sin, for against them they must always fight in thought and in deed until they have gained the mastery over them; and that shall never be complete in this life as long as one bears and feels this image.

I do not deny that a soul may through grace have the upper hand over this image, to such an extent that he or she shall not follow or consent to its irrational stirrings; but to be so completely delivered from this image that one should not feel temptation, or the jabbering of any carnal affection or vain thought at any time – no one can have that in this life.

Reforming in feeling and in faith

✳

This reforming is in faith, as I have said before, and it can be had easily; but after this comes reforming in faith and feeling, which may not be so easily acquired, but through long toil and great effort. Reforming in faith is common to all chosen souls, though they are only in the lowest degree of charity; but reforming in feeling pertains especially to such souls as can come to the state of perfection.

That cannot be had suddenly: but a soul can come to it after great abundance of grace and great spiritual labor, and that is when he or she is first healed of their spiritual sickness, when all bitter passions, carnal pleasures, and other old feelings are burnt out of the heart with the fire of desire, and new gracious feelings are brought in, with burning love and spiritual light: then a soul draws near to perfection and to reforming in feeling.

Desire more grace

It is a wonder to me, since grace is so good and so profitable, why someone having only a little of it – yes, so little that he could not have less, will say, 'Ho! I don't want any more of this, for I have enough.' At the same time I see that a secular person with far more worldly goods than he needs will never say, 'Ho! I have enough, I want no more of this.' But he will always crave more and more, toiling with all his faculties and all his powers, and will never stop coveting until he can have more. Much more then should a chosen soul crave spiritual goods, which are everlasting and make a soul blessed.

Don't hinder yourself

✳

Some people at the beginning of their turning to God set themselves in a certain kind of exercise, whether of body or of spirit, and always keep to that way of working, and not to change it for any other, even though it were better. For they suppose that practice always to be best for them. Therefore they rest in it, and so bind themselves to it by habit that when they have completed it they feel wonderfully at ease, thinking they have done a great thing for God; and if it happens by chance that they are hindered from their custom, they are angry and despondent – even though it may be for a reasonable cause – and their conscience is troubled as if they had done a great mortal sin.

These people hinder themselves from feeling more grace, for they make an end in the middle of the way, where there is no end; for which reason if someone founds his perfection on a bodily or spiritual work that he or she feels at the beginning of their turning to God and wants to seek no further, but always to rest there, they seriously hinder themselves. For that is a feeble craft in which an apprentice has the same skill at all times and which he knows as much of on the first day as he does twenty winters later.

Great diligence is required

There is no special task through which alone a soul might become reformed in faith and feeling, but it is chiefly through the grace of our Lord Jesus. Since our Lord Jesus himself is the special master of this craft and he is the special healer of spiritual sickness. It is therefore reasonable that as he teaches and stirs, so a person follows and works. But it is a simple master who has the skill to teach his pupil only one lesson all the time he is learning, and only a foolish doctor who tries to heal all diseases with one medicine; therefore our Lord Jesus teaches various lessons to his disciples according to their proficiency in learning; and to different souls he gives various medicines to suit the sickness that they feel.

No created being can deserve to have him by their own sole effort, for even if a person could labor as hard in body and spirit as all the creatures that ever existed, they could not by their works alone deserve to have God as their reward. Although a soul works all their life with all their skill and strength, they shall never have a perfect love of Jesus until our Lord Jesus freely gives it.

The example of a pilgrim

There was a man wanting to make a pilgrimage to Jerusalem. Since he did not know the way he came to another man who he knew it and asked whether he could reach that city. The other man told him, 'Whatever you hear, see or feel that would hinder you on your way, do not willingly stay with it, and do not tarry for it, taking rest; do not look at it, do not take pleasure in it, and do not fear it; but always go forth on your way and think that you want to be in Jerusalem. For that is what you long for and what you desire, and nothing else but that.

'If men rob you, strip you, beat you, scorn you and despite you, do not fight back if you want to have your life, but bear the hurt that you have and go on as if it were nothing, lest you come to more harm. In the same way, if people want to delay you with stories and feed you with lies, trying to draw you to pleasures and make you leave your pilgrimage, turn a deaf ear and do not reply, saying only that you want to be in Jerusalem. And if people offer you gifts and seek to enrich you with worldly goods, pay no attention to them; always think of Jerusalem.'

The best spiritual work

Now that you are on the road and know the name of the place you are bound for, begin to go forward on your journey. Whatever spiritual work it is that you should do, in body or in spirit, if it helps this grace-given desire that you have to love Jesus, making it more whole, easier and more powerful for all virtues and all goodness, that is the work I consider the best. Whether it be prayer, meditation, reading or working. As long as the task most strengthens your heart and your will for the love of Jesus and draws your affection and your thought farthest from worldly vanities, it is good.

If it happens that the savor of it becomes less through use, and you feel that you savor another kind of work more, and you feel more grace in another, take another and leave that one. For though your desire and yearning of your heart for Jesus should always be unchangeable, nevertheless the spiritual practices that you are to use in prayer or meditation to feed and nourish your desires may be diverse and may well be changed according to the way you feel disposed to apply your own heart through grace.

Fire and sticks

For it goes with spiritual works and desire as it does with a fire and sticks. The more sticks are laid on the fire, the greater is the flame, and so the more varied the spiritual work that anyone has in mind for keeping his or her desire whole, the more ardent shall be their desire for God. Therefore notice carefully what spiritual work you best know how to do and what most helps you to keep whole this desire and do that. Do not bind yourself to practices of your own choosing that hinder the freedom of your heart to love Jesus. I shall tell you which customs are always good and need to be kept.

A particular custom is always good to keep if it consists in getting virtue and hindering sin, and that practice should never be left. But the practice of any other thing that hinders a better work should be left when it is time. For instance, if somebody has the custom of saying so many prayers or meditating in a certain way for a particular length of time or waking or kneeling for a certain time, or doing other work, this practice is to be left off sometimes when a reasonable cause hinders or else if more grace comes from another quarter.

Do not believe them

✳

Beware of enemies that will be trying to put out of your heart that desire and that longing that you have for the love of Jesus, and to drive you home again to the love of worldly vanity. These enemies are principally carnal desires and vain fears that rise out of your heart to hinder your desire for the love of God. Whatever it may be that they say, do not believe them, but keep on your way and desire only the love of Jesus. Always give this answer: I am nothing, I have nothing; I desire nothing, but the love of Jesus alone.

If your enemies speak to you by strings in your heart, that you have not made a proper confession, or that there is some old sin hidden in your heart that you do not know and never confessed, and therefore you must turn home again, leave your desire and go to make a better confession: do not believe this saying, for it is false and you are absolved. Trust firmly that you are on the road, and you need no more ransacking of your confession for what is past: keep on your way and think of Jerusalem.

Hindrances

✳

For as long as you allow your thoughts to run willingly all over the world to consider different things, you notice few hindrances; but as soon as you draw all your thoughts and yearnings to one thing alone – to have that, to see that, to know that and to love that and that is only Jesus, then you may well feel many painful hindrances. Hindrances both pleasant or painful, bitter or sweet, agreeable or dreadful, glad or sorrowful that would draw down your thought and your desire from the love of Jesus to worldly vanity.

Think nothing of it, do not willing receive it, and do not linger over it too long. But if it concerns something that ought to be done for yourself or your fellow Christian, finish with it quickly and bring it to an end so that it does not hang on your heart. If it is some other thing that is not necessary, or does not concern you, do not trouble about it, do not argue with it, and do not get angry; neither fear it nor take pleasure in it; but promptly strike it out of your heart.

Two lights

You shall understand that there are two lights. The first is a false light; the second is a true light. The false light is the love of this world that a person has in themselves through sin. The true light is the perfect love of Jesus felt in a person's soul through grace. Then whoever perceives and sees the love of this world to be false and failing and is therefore ready to forsake it and seek the love of God, cannot at once feel the love of him but has to abide a while in the night.

The night is nothing but a separation and a withdrawal of the thought of the soul from earthly things, by great desire and yearning to love, see and feel Jesus and the things of the spirit. This is a good night and a luminous darkness, for it is a shutting out of the false love of this world, and it is a drawing near to the true day of the love of Jesus. Nevertheless, this night is sometimes painful and sometimes it is easy and comforting. Therefore it is called night and darkness, inasmuch as the soul is hidden from the false light of the world and does not yet have the full feeling of true light but is awaiting the blessed love of God which it desires.

The hill

For although your soul may be in this restful darkness without being troubled by worldly vanities, it is not yet where it should be; it is not yet all clothed in light, or wholly turned into the fire of love. It well feels there is something above itself that it does not know and does not yet have, but it wants to have it and ardently yearns for it: and that is nothing else but the sight of the city of Jerusalem.

This city signifies the perfect love of God set on the hill of contemplation, which appear to the soul that is outside toiling toward it in desire; by touching of contemplation, a soul sees well that there is such a thing, but he or she does not see what it is in inside. Nevertheless, if one can come inside the city of contemplation, then they see much more than what they saw at first.

The dark house

Whoever will hide from the love of the world and cannot quickly feel the light of spiritual love let them not despair or turn again to the world; but hope in our Lord and lean upon him, that is trust in God and hold fast to him by desire and abide awhile; and that person shall have light. For it happens to that person as it does as if a man has been a great while in the sun and afterward comes suddenly into a dark house where no sun shines. At first he shall be as if blind, seeing nothing at all.

Yet, if he will wait a while he shall soon be able to see around him: first large things and then small ones, and later all that is in the house. It is just the same spiritually. For a man or woman who forsakes the love of the world and comes to themselves in their own conscience, it is at first rather blind in their spiritual sight; but if this man or woman keeps up the same will to love of Jesus, with diligent prayer and frequent meditation, they shall afterward be able to see both large and small things that at first they did not recognize.

The inner eye

As Jesus illuminates the reason through his blessed light he opens the inner eye of the soul, to see him and know him; not all at once, but little by little at different times. The soul does not see *what* God is, for no created being can do that in heaven or earth and the soul does not see God *as* he is, for that sight is only in the glory of heaven. But the soul sees *that* God is: an unchangeable being, a supreme power, supreme truth, supreme goodness, a blessed life, and an endless beatitude. This the soul sees through an understanding which is strengthened and illuminated by the gift of the Holy Spirit.

Although this sight may be only little and for a short time, it is so excellent and so strong that it draws to itself and ravishes the entire affection of the soul from the consideration and awareness of all earthly things, to rest in it forever if it could. And from this kind of seeing and knowing the soul grounds all its inward practices in all the affections, for then it fears God in man as truth, wonders at him as power, and loves him as goodness.

More love

There is no state above the second reforming that a soul can come to here in this life; for this is the state of perfection, and the way toward heaven. Nevertheless, not all the souls that are in this state are equally far advanced. For some have it little, briefly, and seldom; and some longer, clearer and more often; and some have it clearest and longest of all, according to the abundance of grace – and yet all these have the gift of contemplation.

For the soul does not have the perfect sight of Jesus all at once, but first a little, and after that it becomes proficient and comes to more feeling; and as long as it is in this life it can grow more knowledge and in this love of Jesus.

And indeed I do not know what should be more desirable for such a soul that has felt a little of it than to leave and utterly disregard everything else and aim at this alone: to have a clearer sight and purer love of Jesus, in whom is all the blessed Trinity. This way of knowing Jesus, as I understand, is the opening of heaven to the eye of a pure soul, of which holy men speak in their writings.

God above

God is above all material and spiritual creatures: not by the placing of his position but through the subtlety and dignity of his unchangeable and blessed nature. Therefore whoever wants to seek God wisely, and to find him, is not to run out with their thought as if one would climb above the sun, pierce the firmament and form an image of the majesty something like the light of a hundred suns: one should rather draw down the sun and all the firmament and forget it, and cast it beneath where one stands, setting at nought all this and every material thing as well. Let one then think spiritually – if they know how – both of themselves and of God.

If they do so, then the soul sees about itself; and then it sees heaven. This word within is to be understood in the same way. It is commonly said that a soul shall see our Lord within all things, and within itself. It is true that our Lord is within all creatures, but not in the way that a kernel is hidden inside the shell of a nut, or as a little bodily thing is held inside another big one. But God is within all creatures as holding and keeping them in their being, through the power of his own blessed nature.

Sweet letters

Jesus is infinite power, wisdom and goodness, righteousness, truth, holiness and mercy; all this is expressed in holy scripture, and there it is seen by a soul, with all other attributes that go with it. You must know that such gracious intuitions in holy scripture – or any other book made through grace – are nothing else but sweet letters, sent between Jesus the true lover and the souls loved by him.

He has love of very great tenderness for all his chosen children. God comforts them by his letters of holy scripture, drives out of their hearts heaviness and impatience, doubts and fears, and makes them glad and joyful in him, truly believing in all his promises and humbly awaiting the fulfilment of his will.

Liturgical Materials for Hilton's Feast Day

✿ ✿
✿

For use on Walter Hilton's Feast Day, 24 March, or other appropriate occasions:

Walter Hilton of Thurgarton
Mystic, Canon, 1396

Walter Hilton is one of a small group of fourteenth-century mystics that comprise a period in the history of spirituality sometimes called the 'Golden Age of English Mysticism'. Julian of Norwich, another mystic associated with this 'golden age' was a near contemporary of Hilton. It appears she was familiar with some of his ideas. Hilton's writings on prayer and the spiritual life were immensely influential in England in the fourteenth and fifteenth centuries. Hilton was read by laity and clergy, as well as those in monasteries. His most famous works are *The Scale of Perfection,* where he provides spiritual direction to an anchoress and *The Mixed Life,* where Hilton is addressing the situation of a man of influence with familial and professional responsibilities.

Hilton was born around the year 1340. Little is

known about his early life. Later he studied canon law at Cambridge. Eventually, he abandoned the practice of law in order to dedicate his life to prayer, devotion, and contemplation. This eventually led him to join the community of Augustinian Canons in the village of Thurgarton, not far from Southwell. He died there on the eve of the Annunciation on March 24 in the year 1396. In the *Scale of Perfection* he writes, 'For what is a man but his thoughts and loves?' Hilton's spiritual guidance encourages careful self-reflection as well as a cultivation of a holy desire to experience more of the love of God. In the *Mixed Life* Hilton writes, 'The more desire that you have toward him, the more is this fire of love within you.' Hilton quotes Hebrews 12:29 to explain: 'For our God is a consuming fire.'

In addition to the above one or more passages from this volume may be read.

Collect:

Almighty God, Holy Trinity, thou didst reveal to thy servant, Walter Hilton, thine mysteries of perfect love, may we, following his example, find our faith kindled with fire and our spiritual eyes opened to thy glory, through Jesus Christ our Lord, the lover of our souls, who liveth and reigneth with thee and the Holy Spirit one God, now and ever. Amen.

or

Almighty God, Holy Trinity, you revealed to your servant, Walter Hilton, the mysteries of your perfect love, may we, following his example, find our faith

kindled with fire and our spiritual eyes opened to
your glory, through Jesus Christ our Lord, the lover of
our souls, who lives and reigns with you and the Holy
Spirit, one God, now and forever. Amen.

Post Communion:

Almighty God, who graciously made us according
to thy image, by the power of thy Holy Spirit reform
us in faith and feeling, that we, having celebrated the
mysteries of thy Son's Body and Blood, may like thy
servant Walter Hilton, grow in thy grace and abound
in thy love. Amen.

or

Almighty God, who graciously made us according to
your image, by the power of your Holy Spirit reform
us in faith and feeling, that we, having celebrated the
mysteries of your Son's Body and Blood, may like your
servant Walter Hilton, grow in your grace and abound
in your love. Amen.

Psalm	Lessons
46	Genesis 1:26–27; Ephesians 3:14–21; Matthew 7:24–25

Pilgrimage in the Lands of Hilton

Walter Hilton lived, ministered, and died as a member of the Augustinian priory in Thurgarton. The existing building, on the site of the original priory, includes architectural elements from Hilton's time in the fourteenth century. The Priory Church of St Peter is a beautiful historic church, located in a peaceful and idyllic setting. There is a memorial to Walter Hilton on one of the pillars in the nave, done by a local artist as part of a celebration marking the 600th anniversary of Hilton's death in 1996. This rendition of Hilton is suitable for those wishing to mark their visit to the holy place by 'taking a picture' with the saint who once worshipped within the church's walls. The priory church is accessible from the main road, about five minutes by car from Southwell. It is recommended to make the pilgrimage to the priory church by foot. This can be done from Southwell Minster, by taking walking paths through lovely pastoral landscapes.

Maps are available online from the British Pilgrimage Trust. Contact the vicar of St Peter's for access to the interior of the church. Pilgrims may wish to stay or visit Sacrista Prebend. Sacrista Prebend is a retreat house in Southwell, across from the Minster. Sacrista has helped to keep Hilton's witness alive in many ways, including by naming a room after him. The Minster was founded around the year 1000. In 1884 the Minster became the cathedral of the local Anglican diocese and today is the cathedral for the Diocese of Southwell and Nottingham. In the fourteenth century, the Minster, like the Priory in Thurgarton, was a significant centre. It is likely Hilton made the hour walk to the Minster on more than one occasion during his years in Thurgarton. The walking pilgrimage can be done in either direction. Visitors are encouraged to begin or conclude their journey in one of the chapels or altars in the Minster. The Minster gift shop and cafe is nearby.

A Prayer for Making Pilgrimage to Thurgarton

Almighty God, who inspires the desires of *our* hearts to embrace the pilgrim's way. Protect us during our journey, inspire us during our journey, and bring us to that quiet place in the village of Thurgarton where Walter Hilton lived, ministered, and died. May the fire of your love kindle our faith, assuage our doubts, and grant us guidance about the matters that occupy our minds and when, having finished this portion of our earthly pilgrimage, strengthen us for the roads ahead, through Jesus Christ our Lord, who is Himself, our final pilgrimage destination, the true Jerusalem, who lives and reigns with you and the Holy Spirit, one God, now and forever. Amen.

A message from the publisher

If you would like to learn more about the life and spiritual teaching of Walter Hilton, you will be interested to know that Fr Kevin Goodrich OP is writing an accessible introduction to Hilton, to be published in the summer of 2023. The book will introduce readers to the English mystical tradition and the spiritual counsel of Hilton, not as disinterested observers, but as apprentices of the Spirit. You will be invited to make your life a pilgrimage, learning from the wisdom of a trusted guide, whose teachings reflect not only his own education and experience but the venerable tradition of medieval English spirituality.

Also available from
Darton, Longman and Todd:

Enfolded in Love is a collection of books of short, daily devotional readings drawn from the writings of some of Christian mystics who have brought comfort, hope and spiritual insight to millions of people over the centuries.

Julian of Norwich: Enfolded in Love
Daily readings of love,
forgiveness and joy

Julian of Norwich: In Love Enclosed
Daily readings of vision,
compassion and hope

Thérèse of Lisieux: By Love Alone
Daily readings of the 'Little Way'
of love, trust and surrender

Teresa of Avila: Living Water
Daily readings of poverty, union
and mission

DARTON·LONGMAN+TODD